LEARNING ABOUT DOGS

THE BOXER

BY CHARLOTTE WILCOX

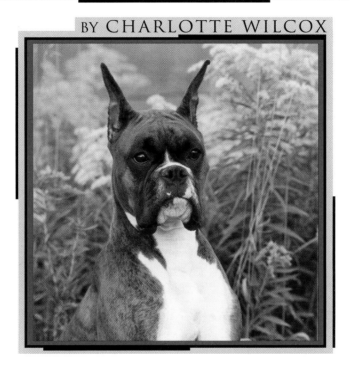

Consultant:
Stephanie Abraham
Life Member
American Boxer Club

CAPSTONE
HIGH-INTEREST
BOOKS

an imprint of Capstone Press
Mankato, Minnesota

Capstone High-Interest Books are published by Capstone Press
151 Good Counsel Drive, P.O. Box 669, Mankato, Minnesota 56002
http://www.capstone-press.com

Library of Congress Cataloging-in-Publication Data
Wilcox, Charlotte.
The boxer/by Charlotte Wilcox.
   p. cm.—(Learning about dogs)
   Includes bibliographical references (p. 45) and index.
   ISBN 0-7368-0762-4
   1. Boxer (Dog breed)—Juvenile literature. [1. Boxer (Dog breed). 2. Dogs.
3. Pets.] I. Title. II. Series.
SF429.B75 W56 2001
636.73—dc21   00-009822

Summary: Discusses the history, development, habits, uses, and care of Boxers.

Editorial Credits
Leah K. Pockrandt, editor; Lois Wallentine, product planning editor; Timothy Halldin,
   cover designer and illustrator; Katy Kudela, photo researcher

Photo Credits
Cheryl A. Ertelt, 19, 21
Daniel Johnson, 14
Jean M. Fogle, 32
Kent and Donna Dannen, 38
Mark Raycroft, cover, 1, 4, 6, 10, 13, 16, 22, 25, 29, 30, 40–41
Norvia Behling, 9, 34, 37
Visuals Unlimited/Cheryl A. Ertelt, 26

1 2 3 4 5 6 06 05 04 03 02 01

TABLE OF CONTENTS

Quick Facts about the Boxer

Description

Height: Most Boxers are 21 to 25 inches (53 to 64 centimeters) tall. Height is measured from the ground to the withers. The withers are the tops of the shoulders.

Weight: Most Boxers weigh between 55 and 80 pounds (25 and 36 kilograms).

Physical features: Boxers are squarely built, muscular dogs. The head is in proportion with a short nose and flat cheeks. The tail and ears usually are cropped.

| **Color:** | Boxers can be fawn or brindle colored. They have a black mask on the face. Most Boxers have white markings. Some Boxers are all or mostly white. These dogs cannot be used for showing or for breeding show-quality dogs. But they still make good pets. |

Development

Place of origin:	Boxers came from Germany.
History of breed:	Boxers descended from large hunting and herding dogs of ancient Asia. These dogs later came to Europe where they were crossed with the English Bulldog.
Numbers:	In 1999, the American Kennel Club registered 34,998 Boxers. In 1999, the Canadian Kennel Club registered 1,695 Boxers. Owners who register their Boxers record their dogs' breeding records with an official club.
Uses:	Many Boxers in North America are family pets. Some are watchdogs, military and police dogs, or guide and service dogs.

CHAPTER 1

THE BOXING DOG

Boxers probably were named after human boxers. Human boxers fight with their fists for sport. Boxer dogs use their front paws to play with other dogs. This playful action resembles the movements of human boxers. That may have been how the breed got its name.

Boxer Relatives

Boxers are related to Bulldogs. Boxers are much taller than modern Bulldogs. But they have some of the same qualities as Bulldogs. Both breeds do not give up when they want something. They also do not seem to be afraid of people or other animals.

People sometimes mistake Boxers for Pit Bull Terriers or Staffordshire Terriers. Some

Boxers have physical traits that are similar to other breeds such as Bulldogs.

people think Pit Bull Terriers are fierce. Boxers look enough like Pit Bull Terriers to make many people afraid of them.

But Boxers are not fierce. They are not known for attacking or fighting with humans. But Boxers may fight with other dogs. This also makes some people afraid of Boxers.

Boxers as Pets

Boxers make good family pets. They are among the most affectionate of all dog breeds. They are faithful to their owners. They especially seem to enjoy being around children. Boxers also learn to accept other pets if they get used to them at a young age.

Boxers are good house dogs for many reasons. They have a short coat. They are easy to house train and are naturally clean. They learn quickly and usually are obedient after they are trained.

Boxers also are good watchdogs. They protect their yard and family when a new person

Boxers are active, playful dogs.

approaches. They will bark to signal a stranger's arrival. But Boxers are not attack dogs.

Boxers are popular family pets because of their many good qualities. Boxers are among the top 10 most popular dog breeds in both the United States and Canada.

CHAPTER 2

THE BEGINNINGS OF THE BREED

The first true Boxers came from Germany. But the breed's beginnings were much earlier and much farther away.

The Mastiffs

Boxers are similar in appearance to a group of dogs called Mastiffs. People brought these dogs to southern Europe from Asia thousands of years ago. Mastiffs are large and strong. People used them for hunting, herding livestock, guarding homes, and fighting in wars.

During the Middle Ages (A.D. 500 to 1500), Mastiffs became popular in northern Europe. There, they were bred with other dogs for hunting purposes.

Boxers originated in Germany.

The Bullenbeisser

Europeans crossed Mastiffs with terriers and other breeds to produce smaller, faster dogs. One such crossbred dog was the Bullenbeisser. This German word means "bull biter."

Hunters used the Bullenbeisser to hunt large game such as bears and wild boars. The dogs had the strength and determination to hold down wild animals until the hunters arrived. The dogs used their front paws to fight and play.

By the 1700s, the Bullenbeisser was popular with German noblemen. These wealthy Germans kept large packs of Bullenbeissers for hunting. They valued the Bullenbeisser for its intelligence and hunting skill.

A New Job and a New Name

By the early 1800s, life in Germany was changing. Some of the noblemen lost their hunting lands in wars. The forests with large

Eventually, the Bullenbeisser became known as the Boxer.

game began to disappear as people cleared land for cities and farms. The loss of their habitat caused many large game animals to die out or leave. People no longer needed the Bullenbeisser for hunting.

But Germans still kept Bullenbeissers. The dogs were more than hunters. The

Boxers like to use their front paws to play.

Bullenbeisser was popular for its personality and appearance. Germans thought the Bullenbeisser was smart, affectionate, and strong. Some owners used the Bullenbeisser to herd cattle. Other owners wanted the dogs as family pets. Some owners took their dogs with them to fight in wars. The dogs often guarded prisoners. The Bullenbeisser also sometimes used its hunting skills to catch enemy soldiers.

Eventually, people started calling the Bullenbeisser the Boxer. Boxer means the same in German as in English. The breed later became popular in Germany, Belgium, and France.

In the 1800s, the Bullenbeisser was crossed with the English Bulldog. At that time, the English Bulldog resembled a Mastiff-type of dog. The modern Boxer is based on the result of this cross.

CHAPTER 3

THE DEVELOPMENT OF THE BREED

By the late 1800s, dog breeding and showing were popular activities in Europe. In 1896, a group of Germans who liked Boxers formed the German Boxer Club. The group held its first dog show that year. German Boxer Club members wanted to work together to improve the breed.

Line Breeding

Breeders usually mate dogs that come from different lines or families. These dogs' qualities may be somewhat different. For example, one line of dogs may be smart but not very attractive. Another line may be better looking but not as easy to train. Most offspring would inherit a combination of qualities from both sides.

Breeding an animal to a close relative is called line breeding. Breeders use this method to breed

Breeders breed dogs that have desirable qualities.

desired features in animals' offspring. The offspring receive features from each parent.

Breeders use line breeding to pass on a good combination of qualities. Line breeding does not pass qualities from other lines to the offspring. This breeding method gives the offspring a better chance of inheriting all of the desired features.

Flora's Story

Around 1886, a German dog breeder named George Alt bought a female Boxer named Flora. Flora was born in Belgium. Flora's coat was tan with black hairs mixed through it. Alt saw that Flora had many desired qualities. He hoped that she would pass on these qualities to her puppies.

Alt brought Flora home to Munich, Germany. He bred her with a local male Boxer. One of the puppies from that litter was named Box. He was tan with white markings. Alt decided to breed Box with his mother once the dog was grown.

Changes in the Breed

Alt used line breeding to make sure Flora's offspring would inherit the features that he

Breeders sometimes use line breeding to achieve desired traits in their dogs.

wanted. He bred Box to his mother. The resulting puppies had all of the qualities that Alt wanted. Alt kept two female puppies from this litter. Alt named these puppies Flora II and Schecken.

Alt later bred Flora II to Box. He bred Schecken to a white Bulldog from an English line. Alt used line breeding with Flora II to keep the qualities that he wanted. Schecken's breeding to the Bulldog introduced new qualities into the breed.

Many of Flora and Box's offspring became champion show dogs. In 1904, Schecken's puppy Flocki was the first Boxer registered by the German Boxer Club. Boxer owners recorded their dogs' breed lines with this club. People from many European countries soon were buying Boxer puppies.

Another famous line of Boxers was the Vom Dom Boxers. The Vom Dom Boxers were developed in Germany by Philip and Friederun Stockmann from 1911 to 1972. The Stockmanns produced many famous dogs. They also helped to create a distinct physical appearance in the breed. Some of the Stockmanns' best dogs were sent to the United States. Boxer breeders in the United States valued these dogs.

Boxer Clubs

People brought Boxers to North America in the early 1900s. The American Boxer Club began in 1935. The Boxer Club of Canada began in 1947.

Dog clubs approve the breed standard for various breeds. The breed standard includes a

Judges use breed standards to judge Boxers in dog shows.

breed's ideal height, weight, colors, and other features. It explains the appearance of the breed. Judges use the breed standard to judge dogs in dog shows. These clubs also keep track of the dog registry for each recognized breed. In 1999, the American Kennel Club (AKC) registered 34,998 Boxers. The Canadian Kennel Club (CKC) registered 1,695 Boxers in 1999.

CHAPTER 4

THE BOXER TODAY

Today, Boxers are one of the most popular breeds in North America. One reason for the breed's popularity is that the dogs get along well with children. Another reason is that they are protective without being fierce or dangerous.

The Boxer's Appearance

Boxers are medium-sized dogs. They are sleek and muscular. Their coats are short and smooth. Their square-shaped bodies appear strong and graceful. Their tails usually are cut short. Boxers hold their tails high.

Male Boxers stand 22.6 to 25 inches (57.4 to 64 centimeters) tall. Height is measured from the ground to the withers.

Boxers are protective of their homes and families.

The withers are the tops of the shoulders. Males weigh between 65 and 80 pounds (29 and 36 kilograms). Females are 21 to 23.6 inches (53 to 59.9 centimeters) tall. They weigh between 55 and 70 pounds (25 and 32 kilograms).

Boxers have blunt muzzles. They have short noses and dark brown eyes. The ears naturally fold down. But owners often have their Boxers' ears cropped. Cropped ears stand up. Many owners believe this helps the dogs hear better. They also believe it helps prevent ear problems.

Some people do not like ear cropping. This group of people includes some veterinarians. These doctors believe ear cropping is unnecessary. Many European countries do not allow ear cropping. But ear cropping is allowed in the United States and Canada. The AKC and CKC include cropped ears as part of their Boxer breed standards.

Boxers' ears naturally fold down. But cropped ears are part of the AKC and CKC breed standards.

Cropped ears also are common for other breeds such as the Doberman Pinscher.

Boxers' Color

Boxers are known for their special coloring. The two main colors are fawn and brindle. Fawn ranges from light tan to red-brown or

White or mostly white Boxers are not used for breeding.

deep brown. Brindle is fawn with black hairs mixed through it. Some brindle Boxers are mostly fawn with dark brindled areas. Others are mostly black with some tan brindled areas.

Boxers can have specific types of markings. Most Boxers have black markings across their face. These markings look like a mask. Many Boxers also have white markings. Boxers with white covering more than one-third of their bodies do not meet the breed standard. They cannot successfully compete in shows.

Some Boxers are born all or mostly white. Some of these dogs are deaf. Dogs with large areas of white have less pigment in their bodies than other dogs. Pigment gives skin, eyes, and hair their color. On white dogs, pigment may be missing from tiny hairs deep inside the ears. Dogs without pigment on these hairs cannot hear.

White or mostly white Boxers pass their lack of pigment on to their puppies. The puppies sometimes inherit the deafness. For this reason, white or mostly white Boxers are not used for breeding. But the majority of white Boxers are as healthy as standard-colored Boxers. Most white Boxers also are not deaf.

Health Concerns

Most young Boxers are strong and healthy. But many Boxers do not live to be very old. Some Boxers do not live more than 10 years. Cancer is common in Boxers. Many Boxers also develop a serious heart condition called cardiomyopathy in their later years.

Boxers can suffer from diseases and other health problems common to large breeds. One problem is a stomach condition called bloat or torsion. The stomach fills with air and becomes twisted. Eating too much food at one time can cause bloat. Drinking water or exercising too soon after eating also can cause this condition. Dogs can die of bloat.

Many large breeds also suffer from problems with their hip joints. The hip joint is not shaped properly in dogs with hip problems. This leads to pain and an inability to walk. This condition is called

Most Boxers are strong and healthy. But some Boxers develop health problems later in life.

hip dysplasia. It is common in large cats and dogs. Dogs with mild hip problems can still be active and healthy. But dogs with hip problems should not be bred because their offspring can inherit this condition.

CHAPTER 5

OWNING A BOXER

Many families choose Boxers for pets. Boxers are playful and seem fond of children. They are affectionate, easy to care for, and easy to handle. But they are spirited, active dogs that need firm training.

Boxers get along well with most people. But they do not always get along with other dogs. Two male dogs together especially is a bad combination. They may fight and be a danger to themselves and people. Boxers will accept pets such as cats if introduced to them at an early age.

Adopting a Boxer

Many people want to adopt Boxer puppies. They may contact an area Boxer club. Club members

Boxers make good family pets.

Boxers enjoy playing with people and other dogs.

help people find a good Boxer breeder who
raises quality dogs.

Boxer breeders sell two kinds of puppies.
These kinds are show-quality puppies and
companion puppies. Owners can compete
with their show-quality puppies in dog
shows. These puppies meet all of the breed
standards. Companion puppies are plain

colored or not quite the right size. But they still make good pets.

Some people prefer to adopt a fully-grown Boxer. People may contact a rescue shelter that cares for homeless dogs. People can adopt dogs from rescue shelters. North American Boxer clubs also offer rescue services for Boxers that need homes. Club members examine the dogs to make sure that they are healthy. The clubs also inform interested people if their dogs are well trained.

Feeding a Boxer

The best food for Boxers is dog food. Pet stores carry several forms of dog food. The most common forms are dry kibble, semi-moist, and canned. Boxers can eat any one of these forms. The most healthful dog food is a good quality kibble that is moistened with warm water.

Adult Boxers may eat 1 pound (.5 kilogram) or more of semi-moist food each day. Most people feed their Boxers twice a day. It is important not to feed Boxers more food than they need.

Some foods are dangerous for dogs. Chocolate can be poisonous for some dogs.

Boxers may eat kibble, semi-moist, or canned dog food.

Dogs also can get sick from spicy or fatty foods. Small or sharp bones are not good for dogs. They can injure dogs' throats and stomachs. Fish and chicken bones especially are unsafe for dogs.

All dogs need plenty of fresh, clean water. They should have water available at all times. Dogs need to be able to drink when they are thirsty.

Grooming

Boxers' short coats require little grooming. They need regular brushing and an occasional bath. Some dogs' toenails get too long and must be clipped. Ears also should be checked and cleaned. Veterinarians can show owners how to perform these grooming tasks.

Boxers need their teeth cleaned regularly. Owners should use a special dog toothpaste and toothbrush. Owners cannot use human toothpaste on dogs because it must be spit out. Dogs cannot spit. Dogs need toothpaste they can swallow.

Older Boxers may get a buildup of plaque on their teeth. This substance can cause tooth decay and gum disease. A veterinarian must use dental tools to remove plaque from dogs' teeth. But this problem is not common to Boxers.

Medical Care

Boxers need a checkup each year to help prevent diseases. At this medical exam, a veterinarian may give vaccinations to the dog. Dogs need these shots of medicine every year to protect them from illness and disease. Veterinarians also may take blood samples to check if the dog has certain diseases.

Veterinarians also will check Boxers for parasites such as heartworms, fleas, ticks, and mites. Owners can give their dogs pills to protect them from heartworms. Mosquitoes carry these tiny worms. They enter a dog's heart and slowly destroy it. Dogs also need a yearly checkup for other types of worms.

Owners must check their Boxers for ticks every day during warm weather. Some ticks carry Lyme disease. This illness can disable or kill an animal or person.

Fleas, lice, and mites are tiny insects that live on a dog's skin. Owners may use collars or apply medicine to their dogs to keep these insects away. Owners should use caution and consult a veterinarian before using these products.

Keeping Boxers Safe

Boxers cannot live outside. Their short coats do not protect them from cold or hot weather. They also need to be close to their owners. Boxers who are separated from their owners seem unhappy. They may get into trouble.

Boxers need plenty of exercise. But Boxers must not be allowed to run freely outside. They

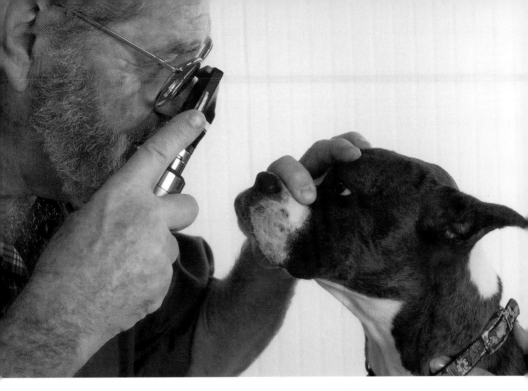

Boxers should have a medical exam each year.

may get into fights with other animals. Boxers need to play in a fenced yard. They must be kept on a leash when outside their yard.

Owners should mark their dogs to identify them if the dogs become lost. Some owners have their telephone number on their dog's collar or tags. Some get their dog tattooed with a patterned mark in the skin. The tattoo is made of tiny ink drops. The tattoo contains an identification number that

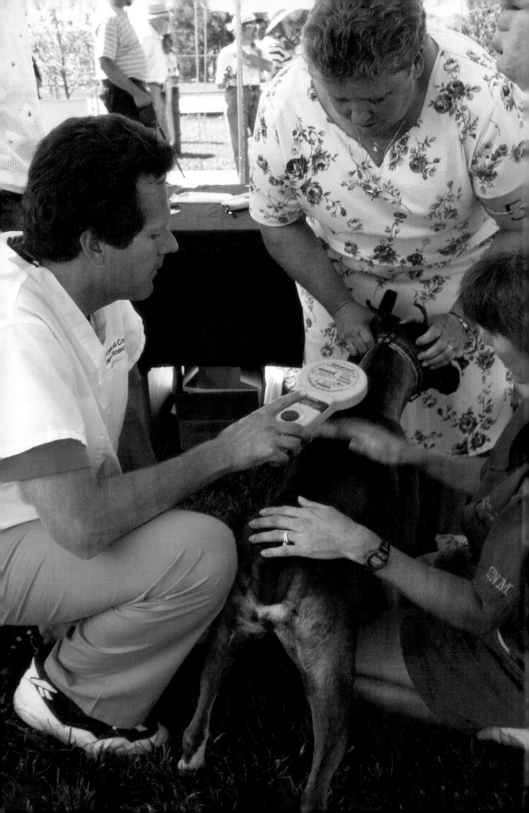

will help locate a dog's owner. It usually is located on the inside of a hind leg.

A microchip is another way to identify dogs. These tiny computer chips are about the size of a grain of rice. A veterinarian surgically inserts the microchip under a dog's skin. The microchip usually is located under the skin on the back of the neck. A veterinarian or shelter worker can scan the microchip if a lost dog is found. The microchip contains the owner's name, address, and telephone number. The microchip also may contain the dog's AKC or CKC registration number.

A healthy Boxer can be a good companion for many years. Boxers may not fit their fighting name. But today, people value them for their affectionate nature.

Veterinarians can scan a dog's microchip to discover information about the dog's owner.

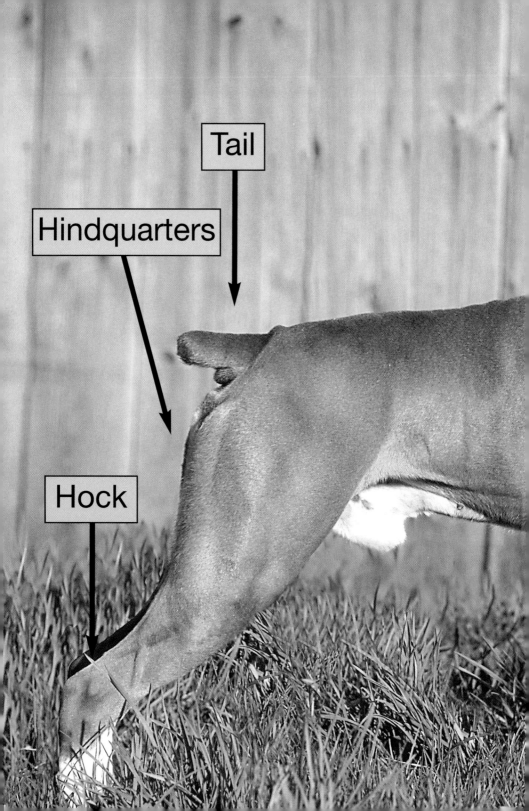

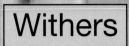
Withers

Ears

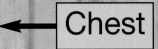
Muzzle

Chest

Forequarters

Quick Facts about Dogs

A male dog is called a dog. A female dog is called a bitch. A newborn puppy is called a whelp until it no longer needs its mother's milk. A young dog is called a puppy until it is 1 year old. A family of puppies born at one time is called a litter.

Origin: All dogs, wolves, coyotes, and dingoes descended from a single wolf-like species. People have trained dogs throughout history.

Types: About 350 official dog breeds exist in the world. Dogs come in different sizes and colors. Adult dogs weigh between 2 pounds (.9 kilogram) to more than 200 pounds (91 kilograms). They range from 5 inches (13 centimeters) to 36 inches (91 centimeters) tall.

Reproduction: Most dogs mature between 6 and 18 months. Puppies are born two months after breeding. A female can have two litters per year. An average litter is three to six puppies. Litters of 15 or more puppies are possible.

Development: Whelps are born blind and deaf. Their eyes and ears open two to three weeks after birth. Whelps try to walk when they are about 2 weeks old. Their teeth begin to come in when they are about 3 weeks old.

Life span: Most dogs are fully grown at 2 years old. With good care, some dogs can live 10 years or longer.

Smell: Dogs have a strong sense of smell. It is many times stronger than a person's sense of smell. Most dogs use their noses more than their eyes and ears. They recognize people, animals, and objects just by smelling them. They may recognize smells from long distances. They also may remember smells for long periods of time.

Hearing: Dogs hear better than people do. Dogs can hear noises from long distances. They also can hear high-pitched sounds that people cannot hear.

Sight: Dog's eyes are farther to the sides of their heads than people's eyes are. They can see twice as wide around their heads as people can. Most scientists believe that dogs can see some colors.

Touch: Dogs seem to enjoy being petted more than almost any other animal. They also can feel vibrations from approaching trains or the beginnings of earthquakes or storms.

Taste: Dogs do not have a strong sense of taste. This is partly because their sense of smell is stronger than their sense of taste. This also is partly because dogs swallow food too quickly to taste it well. Dogs prefer certain types of foods. This may be because they like the smell of certain foods better than the smell of other foods.

Navigation: Dogs often can find their way through crowded streets or across miles of wilderness without guidance. This is a special ability that scientists do not fully understand.

Words to Know

bloat (BLOHT)—a condition in which the stomach fills with air and can become twisted

hip dysplasia (HIP dis-PLAY-zhah)—a hip condition that affects the walking ability of some large dogs and cats

Lyme disease (LIME duh-ZEEZ)—an illness carried by ticks that causes weakness, pain, and sometimes heart and nerve problems

Mastiff (MASS-tif)—a large dog used for hunting, herding, or fighting

register (REJ-uh-stur)—to record a dog's breeding records with an official club

tattoo (ta-TOO)—a word or picture printed onto a person or animal's skin with ink and needles; owners may tattoo an identification number on their dogs.

veterinarian (vet-ur-uh-NER-ee-uhn)—a doctor who is trained to diagnose and treat sick or injured animals

To Learn More

Abraham, Stephanie. *The Boxer: Family Favorite.* New York: Howell Book House, 2000.

American Kennel Club. *The Complete Dog Book for Kids.* New York: Howell Book House, 1996.

Driscoll, Laura. *All about Dogs and Puppies.* All Aboard Books. New York: Grosset & Dunlap, 1998.

Mars, Julie. *Boxers.* Kansas City, Mo.: Andrews and McMeel, 1997.

Mulvany, Martha. *The Story of the Boxer.* Dogs Throughout History. New York: PowerKids Press, 2000.

You can read articles about Boxers in *AKC Gazette, Dog Fancy, Dogs in Canada,* and *Dog World.*

Useful Addresses

American Boxer Club
6310 Edward Drive
Clinton, MD 20735-4135

American Kennel Club
5580 Centerview Drive
Raleigh, NC 27606

Boxer Club of Canada
678 Macharen Drive
Burlington, ON L7N 2Z2
Canada

Canadian Kennel Club
89 Skyway Avenue
Suite 100
Etobicoke, ON M9W 6R4
Canada

Internet Sites

American Boxer Club
http://clubs.akc.org/abc/abc-home.htm

American Kennel Club
http://www.akc.org

Bark Bytes
http://www.barkbytes.com

Boxer Club of Canada, Inc.
http://www.showdogs.org/BCC

Canadian Kennel Club
http://www.ckc.ca

Index